# Designer Scrapbooks
# with April Cornell

# Designer Scrapbooks
# with April Cornell

Sterling Publishing Co., Inc. New York
A Sterling/Chapelle Book

**Chapelle, Ltd., Inc.,** P.O. Box 9252, Ogden, UT 84409
(801) 621-2777 • (801) 621-2788 Fax
e-mail: chapelle@chapelleltd.com
Web site: www.chapelleltd.com

### A Red Lips 4 Courage Book
Red Lips 4 Courage Communications, Inc.
8502 E. Chapman Ave., 303
Orange, CA 92869
*e-mail:* rl4courage@redlips4courage.com
*Web site:* www.redlips4courage.com

### Graphic design of book interior:
*Deborah Kehoe, Kehoe+Kehoe Design Associates, Inc.*
Burlington, VT

### Photography:
*Ryne Hazen, Hazen Imaging*
Ogden, UT

Library of Congress Cataloging-in-Publication Data

Cornell, April.
  Designer scrapbooks with April Cornell.
     p. cm.
  Includes index.
  ISBN 1-4027-1867-5
  1. Photographs--Conservation and restoration. 2. Photograph
albums. 3. Scrapbooks. I. Title.

TR465.C673 2005
745.593--dc22

                                        2004030350

10 9 8 7 6 5 4 3 2 1
Published by Sterling Publishing Co., Inc.
387 Park Avenue South, New York, NY 10016
©2005 by April Cornell
Distributed in Canada by Sterling Publishing
c/o Canadian Manda Group, 165 Dufferin Street
Toronto, Ontario, Canada M6K 3H6
Distributed in Great Britain by Chrysalis Books Group PLC,
The Chrysalis Building,
Bramley Road, London W10 6SP, England
Distributed in Australia by Capricorn Link (Australia) Pty. Ltd.
P. O. Box 704, Windsor, NSW 2756, Australia
Printed and Bound in China
All Rights Reserved

Sterling ISBN 1-4027-1867-5

For information about custom editions, special sales, premium
and corporate purchases, please contact Sterling Special Sales
Department at 800-805-5489 or specialsales@sterlingpub.com.

*"The past can comfort, and help us with reflection, but it can also inspire us and influence our future days."*

—*April Cornell*

The fabrics, clothing, and household accessories designed by artist April Cornell are distinctive because of her use of rich color, pattern, and texture. For more than 30 years, she has translated her delightful combinations of color and floral designs into exquisite collections that are showcased in more than 105 April Cornell and La Cache boutiques throughout North America.

A true sentimentalist, April has kept journals and scrapbooks her entire life. Because her outlook on the world is as unique and artful as she is, her pages are filled with design ideas and techniques never seen before. April's pages have deep dimension—both physically and emotionally—and in this book she will show you how to create the same feeling.

Welcome to her vivid, rich world, and to scrapbooking the April Cornell way.

# table of contents

# Where We've Been, Where We're Going

My life is full of moments that are extraordinary, yet fleeting. Journaling, note taking, collecting, and scrapbooking are my methods for holding memories for the future—to take out and appreciate at my leisure. Through a collected leaf, a dried flower, a newspaper clipping, or a watercolor sketch, a place and time return to me to be savored over and over. Through a dated sketch of the view from the window of a plane, a hotel balcony or a lakeside verandah, I recall a day, a season, a child, or a feeling that was important to me. I savor the flavor of my life.

Many of you may have had an experience similar to one I have had. Some years ago, I was visiting my grandmother at whose house my sisters and I had spent many summer vacations as children. The place is packed with memories of relatives, scents of Cape Breton, Nova Scotia, and the feel of the freedom of holidays. On this return trip, much had changed—no grandfather, no sisters, and no pets. When I opened the back door, I had a vision of our childhood dog, Tiny, and a host of memories came at me in an unbidden rush of surprise.

So it is with journaling and scrapbooking. Through the collecting of items that conjure memories, we can open windows to our personal history. We open doors to the past and the forgotten beauty of our lives.

# Early Scrapbooking Days

The first scrapbook I kept as a child was when the Queen of England came to Canada. She was young and pretty, and color photo after color photo of her appeared in all of the papers. My mother helped me make that first scrapbook, and I can remember other girls making them too. Back then we never gave a second thought to archival methods, and glued images and photographs right to the page. Today there are special adhesives, papers, and scissors. I try not to get so caught up in the science of scrapbooking that I lose the fun of it.

When I was in high school, I kept an album. My mother recently sent it to me and I have enjoyed the pictures of my girlfriends and me. Carefully taped onto the pages were snapshots, restaurant napkins from the A & W, and the McCall's pattern from a corduroy jumper I made when I was in the eighth grade. Twenty-five years later, McCall's asked me to create patterns, and here even more years later, I am creating corduroy jumpers for my customers. Life takes such interesting twists, and with my scrapbooks, I can reflect back on them.

Often we create our pages to share and impress others with. Yet, designing them can be such a personal experience that not only records where we have been, but also gives us time to reflect on where we want to go. It's never too late to start. I don't get worried about being perfectly chronological. I will reach into boxes of photos and memorabilia and put together pages marking long-ago experiences, often gathering like subjects such as Halloween over the years.

*A photo booth snapshot captures my freckled face and the pixie cut that I thought was the height of fashion at the time.*

*Fortunately, I come from a long line of sentimentalists who took photographs throughout my childhood, including this one of my sisters and me. We were a happy bunch!*

*Pajama parties were the rage when I was a young girl and were part of the lesson that good friends are a foundation of life.*

# How I Started Scrapbooking

My parents were from the Maritimes, Cape Breton, Nova Scotia and were the first of their families to leave the area in search of a brighter future. I was born in Montreal, although we moved often because of my father's job as a business executive. My parents had three daughters—of which I am one—and a son.

We lived a three-day drive from extended family. My parents were committed to ensuring we did not miss any warmth or love, and they created an exceptionally cozy home life for us. I may be as sentimental as I am because of the wonderful memories of my childhood.

When I was 9 years old we landed back in Montreal from Toronto. One melancholy day—perhaps between best friends—my mother found me moping over a photo of Toronto friends. She told me to put the picture away and go out to play. I carefully added it to my scrapbook, and did as I was told. I have been squirreling away photos and bits and pieces of places ever since.

I love to keep a little piece of wherever I have visited tucked away in a journal; a twig, a flower, a scrap of fabric, a newspaper clipping, or just some written notes. I started scrapbooking by detailing shopping trips with girlfriends downtown—my first pairs of bell bottoms, Ann Landers columns—all precursors to my years of collecting. To this day, I gather clippings, menus, and notes from special friends to mix with photographs. They may not always get right into a book; I keep them in hat boxes or baskets until my personal muse calls me to put them together. Eventually the pages get done, and I enjoy the process.

*My mother is an amateur artist and she inspired me to pursue using my talents. Like me, she uses little paintings to recall memories. Here she painted my sisters and me and jotted the note, "Remember when?"*

*My parents, Florence and Seaton, nicknamed Rusty, created a warm and nurturing home filled with many memories I enjoyed recording in my scrapbooks.*

*I became passionate about scrapbooking in my young teens, about the time of this photo of my seventh grade graduating class. Check out the white pumps!*

*My grandparents, Sadie and Rod MacDonald, were an ever-present source of joy in my young life.*

# A Perfect Partnership and a Plan

My husband, Chris, and I were both born in Montreal, Canada. Both of us are Anglophones, which means English-speaking Quebecers, but the essential French character of our birthplace has wrapped and entwined itself around us to such a degree that we are neither French nor English. Quebec French has become isolated from the Parisian French of Europe, and so has Quebec English developed its own style, one part British English, one part Quebec French, and another part American English. We are a blend. Montreal was a great beginning for our life of travel and appreciation of other cultures and aesthetics.

*Our first shop on the second floor of a Victorian brownstone in Montreal was our beginning. Here Chris and I enjoy some time with Cameron, our first-born son.*

Chris and I met in Montreal at Dawson College. We had a love-at-first-sight sort of relationship, which on my part had a lot to do with his beautiful rust corduroy pants, strawberry blonde hair, and red goatee. I guess it was a color thing!

After college we started a business together. Chris led me to Asia with the plan that we could import things we found on our travels and sell them. We began our life of travel, buying, selling, and of learning skills and growing business in foreign environments.

Our first shop was modest, the second floor of a Victorian brownstone in Montreal. The rent was affordable and we kept our cash in a fishing tackle box. At our first opening, we filled the bathtub with ice and had a champagne and strawberry debut. Since then, it has been one party after another!

Chris has always had a dream of where we could go. We travel often, although not always together. We have made hundreds of thousands of decisions together, and have had many people helping us along the way, but at the center there has always been the two of us and the fishing tackle box!

Scrapbooking our relationship lets me focus on our rich life and love and gives me time to appreciate the great gift I have in my husband.

*Chris teases that once he realized we were in business together he figured we better get married. We did, on a beautiful summer day in 1975, at my parent's home.*

*Chris and I traveled so much that Swissair asked us to pose for a print ad that ran in the international edition of Newsweek. Talk about frequent flyers!*

# Recording My Three Sons

Because travel is such a big part of our lives, my boys, Cameron, Kelly, and Lee, tend to have more pages of themselves in different places than at birthday parties or first days of school. We, as a family, have probably a jet-lag aggregate that would put Rip Van Winkle to shame. We have transit lounge experiences that make us laugh as much as a birthday party. Their growth is marked by where we may have been adventuring at a particular time in their lives.

As a mother, I try to preserve not just the images of the boys, but also the feelings I had at different stages of their development. I hold onto notes and letters I have written to the boys and to ones they have given me. Making copies and adding them to pages helps capture what was on our minds at the time. I also incorporate favorite artwork or doodling. Rather than being sequestered in a box, the drawings can be enjoyed.

On one trip we took, my youngest son, Kelly, had an imaginary friend who was the talk of the trip. I made sure to include a few notes about this friend on the page about the trip so that he would not be forgotten. Some of the things the boys gathered in their pockets over the years, such as beads, make good objects to embellish a page and bring back a memory too.

*As an artist, I often prefer my paints and sketch pad to a camera. Here I caught Kelly reading a book on one of our trips.*

The boys attended school in India while we lived there for a year, so I have been sure to use the rich fabrics of the culture on their pages so they will always remember the beauty of their experiences there. Help your children remember more than just the visuals. Press a small clipping of pine from a trip to the mountains onto a page, or fill a vellum envelope with a bit of rich red soil from a trip to bring alive the smells and feel of what was around your child while growing up.

*The boys grew up all over the globe. In fact, I think those are maps on Lee and Cameron's shirts! I still enjoy catching up on our family memories by going back and working on pages with photos and memorabilia gathered through the years.*

*No matter where we traveled, Kelly was never camera shy.*

*In 1994, we traveled through Nepal with the boys. Chris and I traded being in photographs with Lee and Kelly.*

# Scrapbooking Personal Milestones

Too often we tend to spend our time scrapbooking and journaling the lives of those around us, most often our children, and don't take time for our own personal events. Whether you are a working woman, a community volunteer, a homemaker, or a combination of any of these occupations, you certainly have some milestones worth reflecting on. Taking time to document personal achievements and passions helps us appreciate ourselves as well as gives us a chance to spend time reflecting on what we want to do in the future.

In my case, I enjoy seeing how our company has grown from small beginnings. I also like to mark a favorite collection or a display I was fond of. Surely you have a favorite co-worker you'd like to remember or you have participated in a community event you'd like to recall years from now.

Just as we are coached to take time for our personal health, take some scrapbooking time for yourself too. I like to gather favorite business cards and programs from enjoyable events I have attended in a folder to be put together on a page at a later date. Every woman loves a project. As great as it is to finish something, it is also important that there is something left to do—to anticipate and look forward to, to dream about the "one day when"... the tomorrows.

*In Canada, our stores are named La Cache. Here Chris and I mark the opening of a new store.*

*We are a very hands-on company, and the newest line of clothing hangs on racks in the hallways so everyone working at the main office has access to what is new.*

*The vestibule of our corporate offices in Vermont changes each season, as do the displays in our boutiques. These blue and yellow ensembles greeted summer visitors.*

# Your Personal Creative Space

Because I am in the business of being creative, having an inspiring place to work is very important to me. You'll find that having your own workspace is an important ingredient of your own creativity, especially when scrapbooking. You will have much more spontaneity to be creative if you have your own sacred place to work, particularly if it is in a spot where you do not have to put things away. You want to be able to pick up where you left off, and not go digging for your supplies every time you work. Surround yourself with beautiful things you like to work with. You'll find projects for attractive button jars, ways to hold snippets of ribbon, and a beautiful box for holding embellishments in this book. Taking time to make your workspace special will result in inspiration that will show on your scrapbook pages.

I find that keeping an "inspiration board" works well for me. It is a bulletin board within easy reach of my desk where I gather swatches of fabric, colors, illustrations, and photographs that have caught my eye. I use push pins to hold things in place and move them around as I see a creative vision evolving. You'll find that if you do the same thing with elements you'd like to use on your pages, your scrapbook will begin to take on a depth of expression not seen before.

*This is a color swatch book that I begin my seasonal linens collection with. It has a very scrapbook quality to it.*

*Assembling swatch books is one of the first stages of developing a new line. The same theory works for making decisions about what fabrics to mix together on a scrapbook page.*

*I like to keep an inspiration board close to my desk so I can pin up things that inspire me. This board is on the wall of my office in Delhi.*

*I find the vibrant colors and relaxed style of the tropics to be very inspiring.*

*A garden can be a quick creative retreat. My side-yard garden in Burlington, Vermont provides me with everyday inspiration whether it is in bloom in spring or under snow in the winter.*

# Places of Personal Inspiration

Sometimes it takes a complete change of scenery to become refreshed and inspired. Nature has different palettes and wonders in different places. The Caymans offer me bright pinks, yellows, oranges, and greens set against ocean blue. The Boreal Forest around Bark Lake, Quebec hands me fallen bark and leaves, wildflowers, and the colors in mushrooms to bring into my work. Just about anywhere, including right outside my own door in Burlington, Vermont, there is a garden in which I always find inspiration.

I suggest that the same holds true when you are scrapbooking. Have you even wondered why you finished so many pages when you brought your scrapbooking on a trip? It may go beyond the fact that you were out of your normal routine, and simply be because the change of surroundings sparked new inspiration to be creative.

The next time you have a chance to travel to a new place, consider bringing along a few scrapbooking supplies. There is no need to pack more than a few papers, embellishments, and a pair of scissors. You are likely to find that you create some pretty wonderful pages, and you will enjoy remembering where you were when you put them together.

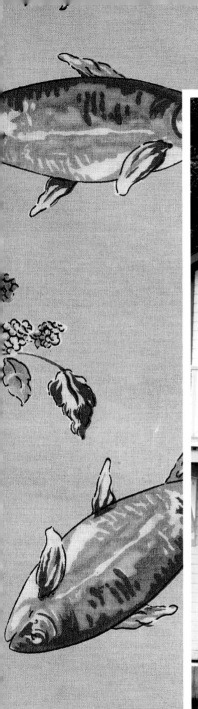

The lapping water at Bark Lake and the surrounding forest is always inspiring to me, whether I am seated on the dock or on a walk under the trees.

# The Rich Fabric of India

When Chris and I first started off to see the world and build our business, we had no idea the role India would play in our lives. It is a country rich in textile history, full of art and craft, that has become a primary source country for our company. We have developed many deep relationships there. We create, manufacture, socialize, explore, and even live there part time.

You will see that much of what I have been exposed to in India makes its way into my work and my scrapbooking. I have absorbed the beauty of color and texture the Indian culture offers.

So much of what we do is created because of the talented Indian artisans who translate my designs into beautiful fabrics and clothing. The ability of our employees to work with vibrant dyes and materials helps give our products their trademark colors and patterns. I have a passion for fabrics, which carries over to my scrapbooking. Throughout this book you will find many ideas for using fabric as an alternative to paper for your pages. Remember, every fabric pattern can become a scrapbook paper when you use a color copier.

*Sometimes it takes getting down on the floor to hammer out a design. There are times when the same is true of my scrapbooking.*

*Vats of vibrant dyes stand ready to be used for the next fabric designs. These colorfast dyes are a mainstay of our fabric business.*

*The staff in our factories works closely with me to translate my ideas and designs into fabrics that will become clothing or home accessories.*

# Giving Back

As India enters the new century with some of the brightest and most creative minds in the world, it still carries with it an underclass of poverty and ignorance. It is a country of a billion people with tolerance and cultural diversity, but outside the walls of our offices and factories is the deep poverty of the slums and remote villages.

Chris and I are involved in The Giving World Foundation and its sister umbrella organization, Concern India. The foundations fund street schools, named the Gali Schools, that serve first-generation learners whose parents may not read or write. The schools prepare the children to be able to move into more advanced schooling. The organizations also fund micro-industries that include raising goats and kitchen gardens.

As you can imagine, we get far more than we give in the smiling faces, a prize vegetable, the voice of the successful reader, the waving hand of the girl student working to be the best in her class, or in the singing voices of the elderly women.

It is all about the hand up, not the hand out. It is about opportunity and human dignity. It is about progress. You'll see some of the people helped by The Giving World Foundation on some of the scrapbook pages in the coming chapters.

*The Indian culture is colorful, vibrant, and tolerant. The people dress in cheerful hues and enjoy the beauty in each day.*

# From Me to You

We are each called upon to use the gifts we have been given. In my case, I am an artist, designer, and illustrator. You'll see that I enjoy including little paintings and pictures on my scrapbook pages. You can enjoy them too. I invite you to use a color copier and make copies of the illustrations I share with you on these pages. Consider them a little gift from me to you.

Remember to enjoy your memories, and happy scrapping!

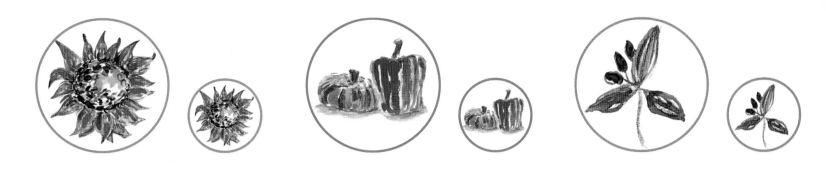

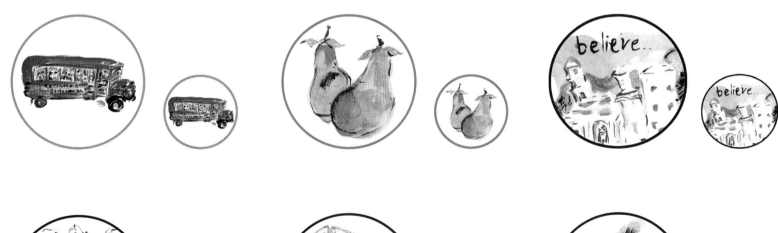

Cameron received Turtie and Turtelina for his 6th birthday. Turtie outlived Turtelina by 13 years. One day Turtie ventured out the back door for his exercise and never came back. He has entered into family lore.....

# chapter one

# Journaling Style

### your scrapbook as a journal

Journals include personal thoughts and, in my case, paintings and drawings.
My scrapbook pages also include poems and verses I have written to help me
remember special times. You can put an even more personal twist on your scrapbooking if you treat your pages like a journal. In this chapter I will show you how.

Mom, Mary & Chris

Bark Lake

We have had many happy family memories at our home at Bark Lake. I like to collect fallen bark, which can easily be written on with a felt marker for page notes. A small painting I did of a young boy complements snapshots of the boys swimming off the dock with Chris. Combining small artwork with photos is a good journaling technique.

GRANDMOTHER

Agenda on the occasion of
Mary Cornell's
80th Birthday. at Bark
Boreal Forest.
Quebec

Aug 15 . meet and greet at . la
Thurs eve !! settle in ci''

Aug 16 .
Fri morn. breakfast at
8:30 - 10 Golf at Aru.
10am- (senior males 16-8
Golf) depart from cott
ladies & junior ma
water activitie
1pm buffet lunch
6:00pm meet at Mother's
6.30 cocktails and

Aug 17- breakfast 9-11 at cottage !.
9-11
water activities all day
buffet lunch.
2-5 Sea Plane Ride (weather permit!!.
7pm Birthday bbq.-cottage one.
Aug 18- TTFN !

aug
16

When Chris' mother, Mary,
turned 80 we gathered at the
lake for a wonderful weekend
celebration. I handwrote plans
for the party and drew some
simple illustrations in pencil.
I copied the sheet, and custom-
ized each person's invitation by
coloring the drawings with water-
colors. For fun, I did a painting
of one of the guest room beds.

*Windows have always had a special meaning to me. They represent the future and opportunities, and are a great symbol for looking back at good memories. I use windows in my illustrations often. Perhaps you have a fondness for doors or other architectural elements you can highlight on a page.*

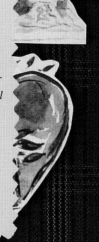

Windows draw me to . . .

## NATURE DOESN'T MATCH – IT COORDINATES

If you see, like I do, nature as a source of all color, you also see that nature doesn't match. Nature's colors vary, but they still belong together. She is the perfect coordinator, and a hapless matcher.

Have you ever worn a matching two-piece outfit and had somebody say to you, "Oh, that is a nice match!" Of course you haven't. They may say, "What a nice match" when the blue of your blouse picks up the blue flowers in your yellow skirt, but matching shades exactly is a thankless exercise. There is no goal other than matching, and there is no reward in the achievement of it. Mostly there is probably a lot of irritation in the accomplishment.

enjoy the

# VIEW

Bearded, the lion: Mike Snowdon, the head gardener at Rowallane Garden, near Belfast, takes his rest amid his horticultural creations

R E P O S E

When I travel, I am constantly recording my surroundings. If something in a local newspaper catches my eye, I often tear it out and tuck it between the pages of my journal. Here a photo of a very content seated Irish man joins a photo of two of my favorite quiet places, including the dock at Bark Lake, and a favorite little illustration of an easy chair.

Reading is a passion Chris and I have tried to pass on to our boys. Rather than worry about being chronological, I pulled together photos of all the boys reading. In this case, we seem to have been successful with Cameron (left) and Lee (top right), but were still working on Kelly (lower right)!

## reading journals

Reading is a wonderful way to escape and relax, and it seems there is always a list of books to share with friends. Then there are the wonderful books friends recommend. A reading journal is the perfect place to keep track of all those book titles.

A spiral-bound journal or guestbook can be embellished in a number of ways. Torn fabric strips can be tied to the spiral wires to dress up the binding. If the cover is not too thick, sew on a fabric covering. Otherwise, a glue gun can be used. Frames, charms, and stick-on letters can be combined with your own illustrations to make a special journal for recording personal book titles.

Take a few minutes to embellish the inside cover with coordinating fabric.

When we travel as a family we accumulate all kinds of paper documents and stubs that are a great record of our family time. Extra passport photos, maps, ticket stubs, and even vaccination reports document where we went, what we looked like, and what we did to prepare for the trip.

☑ Photo
☐ Visa
☐ Passport
☑ Ticket
☐ Money
☐ Travel
☑ Immunize
Let's Go!!

Years ago, while with a good friend, I wandered into a delightful shop in Paris. We had such a wonderful time that I painted a picture and wrote a few verses about the experience. I think it is much more descriptive than a photograph, so I gave it its own special page in my book.

There is a shop where I long to go,
It's pink and petite, and will always be "just so,"
It has a window with a gossamer dress in mint julep green,
There's a wonderful hat, and button-up red shoes,
And a charming salesgirl,
Part diplomat, the other part chanteuse...

MARIE CLAUDE

As a traveler and a birder, I marvel at the birds
...in Delhi
...the Caymans
...Vermont
Quebec

Birds are my fancy, and I watch them wherever I go. They influence my work in many ways. Their feathers make a colorful addition to journal scrapbook pages. A painting of Cayman Parrots adorns the front of a note card. Stationery is a good source for illustrations.

Cayman Parrots

## a birding journal

I am a passionate bird watcher. I find it a wonderful way to stay in touch with my surroundings and the beauty of nature. I keep a record of all of my sightings. A birding journal is easy to make with these materials:

- Two 12" bamboo sticks
- Two 12" x 12" colored card stock scrapbook pages
- Three 3" x 12" strips of colored card stock
- Six 12" x 12" white card stock scrapbook pages
- Sewing machine and thread
- Scissors

Begin with four 12" x 12" white scrapbook pages. Sew one page to each long edge of a 3" x 12" strip of colored card stock at the edge of one strip. Repeat with the other strips and the remaining four white pages. For the front cover, sew a colored 12" x 12" page to the top right side of one set of pages. For the back cover, turn the same set of pages over and sew the other colored sheet to the top left white sheet. Place the other sets of pages inside the cover.

Using a pair of scissors, cut 1/2" slits approximately 2" apart down the center of the binding strips. Cut through all three binding strips. Weave two 12" bamboo sticks in and out of the slits to bind the pages together. Decorate the cover to suit however you'd like to use your journal.

Kelly played a variety of sports and accumulated many team photos, and I wasn't sure how to store them. A page that folds out and acts as a portfolio was the answer.

This page is held shut with a small loop of ribbon hooked around a button sewn to the fabric backing. The inside cover is lined with one of Kelly's grammar school art projects. It's the perfect place to store the many photos he has of his days in organized sports.

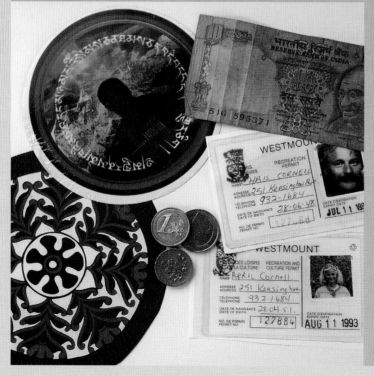

## your scrapbook as a journal

In the past, journals have differed from scrapbooks because they tended to be more casual and include personal thoughts and musings. Your scrapbook pages can become much more personal if you think of them as a place to gather your musings and thoughts as well as some of the papers and little treasures that document your life.

Don't be afraid to sketch, doodle, or draw something that will help you remember an experience or feeling you have had. Hold onto ticket stubs from a favorite show, or a small drawing a child made. Things with dates such as boarding passes help you remember trip details long after you return.

Jot down a favorite saying or a quote from a child to include in your pages. If you enjoy writing poetry or free verse, include some on your pages.

## gathering treasures

A journal-style scrapbook page can also include some of the little beauties of nature. I'll often pick up a colorful fallen bird feather or pick a flower and press it between pages. Sometimes I dry small buds or blooms and tuck those between pages too.

Perhaps you want to remember the smell of freshly mown hay, or you had a wonderful walk in the autumn woods and a fiery changed leaf caught your eye. Whatever it may be, include the treasures of nature on your pages.

One way to dry flowers or grasses is to place them between the pages of a large telephone book and stack another heavy book on top. Leave the piece between the pages for about six weeks before removing.

### protect your originals

There are many reasons why you may not want to cut up original drawings or artwork to include on your pages. Some of the other elements on journal-style pages may not be archival. Good quality color copies are readily available, so there's no need to risk the original piece.

After lots of experimentation, I have found that the best reproduction comes from making a color copy. While scanners are available, it is just an extra step that does not offer a better copy. The only exception to this would be if you wanted to work with the image in a photo-editing program.

### make your own papers

My love of fabrics is obvious, and you may share it too. If you have a favorite fabric, and you would prefer to work with the design in paper, make a copy! Simply lay the fabric on a color copier and duplicate.

For best results, press the fabric first. Then, place a sturdy piece of cardboard under the fabric so that when you place it on the glass surface of the copier there is a solid backing to support the fabric.

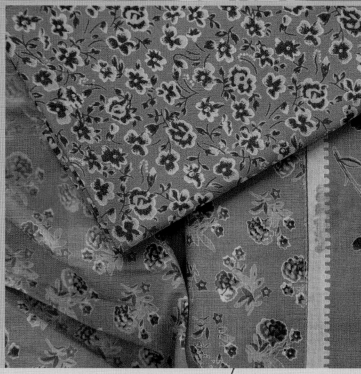

You can create patchwork by combining different patterns on the same copy. Copy the fabric on the largest piece of paper the copier can print so that you will have plenty of image to utilize.

*Fabric brings dimension and texture to a page. Sample pieces and remnants are available at craft and fabric stores. Look for unique fabrics in table runners or napkins on sale that can make attractive focal points for your pages.*

Celebrate

# chapter two

# Fashioned with Fabric

Because I've always loved fabric, and designing fabric is a large part of my life's work, it is no surprise that I like to use it frequently when scrapbooking. I probably use fabric more than traditional scrapbookers use paper. I love the texture and color possibilities it brings to the pages. I'm excited to share some of my techniques with fabric with you!

Boys in suits, slightly large,
Bride in white, pearls and flowers,
Smiles and laughter,
Lace and beads,
Magic wedding day.

Florence marries Jan

Fabric can be layered on a page. Start with a 12" x 12" piece for the background, and then add narrower and narrower bands of contrasting pieces. On this page, the edges of the bands are turned under for a clean look. This page features my mother's second wedding, so a small piece of lace is fashioned into a wedding dress.

Fabric doesn't have to be ironed flat to work on a page. Gather it until you like how it looks. Use a glue gun to hold the folds in place. Small swatches of fabric cut with pinking sheers can add color and additional pattern to the page.

# boys of Summer

When using fabric as the page background, work with heavy card stock. Art supply stores will cut it, if you buy enough quantity. Choose fabrics that can withstand high heat; cotton and linen are best. Use iron-on fusing to adhere the fabric to the board. You can use the fusing for the additional fabrics on the page, or you may prefer a glue gun or gummy adhesive.

**Go!**

**The Home Team**

Scrapbook pages are a great place to use up fabric remnants from other projects. The red fabric was not big enough to cover the 12" x 12" page, so a smaller, contrasting piece is used down the left side of the page. Both pieces are adhered with iron-on fusing, and the buttons are glued using a hot glue gun.

A wood box, large enough to handle 12" x 12" pages, can be decorated and transformed into a showcase for dimensional scrapbook pages. Use your favorite scrapbooking techniques on the top of the box.

## project

### dimensional memories

Scrapbook pages are becoming more and more dimensional, and many won't actually fit into a scrapbook. A decorative wood box that can sit out atop a coffee table is a great way to store pages and make them accessible for everyone to enjoy. It also protects them from potential damage.

An unfinished square wood box, available at craft stores, can be sanded and painted whatever color you choose. Assemble a collage of memories just as you would a scrapbook page. Paper works best for this project. Using a decoupage medium, adhere the cutouts, papers, and images to the top of the box. Metal cutouts can be added after the coating is dry. Rubber stamp whatever wording you would like to personalize the box.

The box will be seen from all angles, so decorate the sides too. For fun, add fabric pockets or a piece of jewelry to one of the sides. To protect the pages in the box, cut pieces of bubble wrap and layer between each page.

A fanciful box like this would make a wonderful gift and is a great way to present a special dimensional page to a friend.

Fabric brings dimension and texture to a page. Sample pieces and remnants are available at craft and fabric stores. Look for unique fabrics in table runners or napkins on sale that can make attractive focal points on your pages.

Pink are the flowers of summer's days,
Rose is the color of baby's cheeks,
Green are the leaves of rose's sweet,
Lime is the tang of the lemonade
Blue is my love and blue is the sky,
Summer so quickly you go by.

A page that highlights favorite foods and recipes is a fun addition to any kitchen when displayed on a small easel.

Sadie's Plum Loaf

raisin teabiscuits

April Cornell
LUXURY CHEF

Stir with a silver spoon,
present with style that
delights the room.

## Home Made Macaroni

makes 4 to 6 servings

1 pound elbow macaroni
3 tablespoons Cabot butter
3 tablespoons Five Roses flour
1 1/2 cups milk
pinch of salt & a pinch of pepper
3 cups Vermont Extra Sharp
Cheddar cheese
1/2 cup bread crumbs
paprika

Cook elbows macaroni as package directs; drain. Preheat oven to 350 degrees. In a medium saucepan, melt butter. Stir in flour. Gradually stir in milk. Cook, stirring constantly over medium heat, until sauce thickens. Stir in salt and pepper. Add cheese; stir until cheese melts. Spoon macaroni and cheese into greased 2 quart baking dish. Top with breadcrumbs and paprika. Bake 30 minutes. Tip: Recipe may be doubled.

# project

## cooking up memories

My husband, Chris, says, "It's always about the food." I do seem to enjoy drawing and painting food when I am not actually eating!

Cloth napkins are great to use on scrapbook pages. They are just the right size to cover a full page and can be cut up for borders and other decorative treatments. The sleeve of a child's dress works just perfectly as a chef's hat. Roll up a small piece fabric to look like a napkin and make a napkin ring with a silk flower and some beads strung on wire.

A favorite recipe to go along with images of favorite foods would be a fun addition to a page. I like to work with copies so I can feel no remorse when I begin cutting and trimming images.

Use a contrasting fabric as a mat around a favorite illustration, and trim it with ribbon. These tropical hues were inspired by our retreat in the Cayman Islands. I love bright sun-kissed colors, and using fabric instead of paper gives pages strong color intensity.

Lazy Cayman Daze.

A chalkboard,
A teacher,
A slate,
Learning is food for the great.

Learning

Teacher and Slate

The Great

Beautiful Indian fabrics showcase photos of one of my favorite causes—the Gali Schools. Run on the streets of the Yamuna Pushta slums in Delhi, the schools provide children with the only organized education they may ever have. The background fabric was adhered to the board with iron-on fusing, while the accent pieces were attached with sticky dots.

A small piece of a sheer scarf adorns the corner of a page featuring drawings and Indian money. To make a see-through pocket for holding collectibles, glue either end of a piece of sheer ribbon to the lower back corners of the page. Use a glue gun to seal the lower portion of the ribbon to the bottom of the page.

Paisley, checks, and polka dots coordinate to make dynamic pages as the colors tie all the patterns together. Small pieces of fabric can have a big impact on a page. As an artist, finding inspiration is key to being able to create. I am always seeking places and things that inspire me, and this page is a reminder of what those things are.

inspire

*A handmade get-well card is a heartfelt wish for a friend, and will be treasured.*

## get-well card and gift tags

As a fabric junkie, it's hard for me to part with even the smallest pieces of fabric. Swatches and remnant pieces are perfect for making personal cards or gift tags. For a card, cut a piece of cardstock or paper the size you'd like the card to be. Score and fold it, and experiment with placing small pieces of fabric in various designs on the front of the card. For gift tags, you can either cut your own or use manila shipping tags available at stationery and office supply stores.

Once you like what you see, lightly tack the fabrics in place with glue. This will keep them in place when you sew them to the card using a sewing machine. Use simple straight or zigzag stitches. Ribbon can be tricky to sew, so to keep the project from getting too complicated, use glue or sticky dots to adhere it to the card or tag. Use rubber stamps in an old typewriter font for the message.

*Gift tags can be easily embellished using small fabric pieces and a sewing machine. The lettering is done using rubber stamps in a vintage typewriter font.*

### *designer tip*

**Common Envelope Sizes**—Keep in mind that unless you want to make your own envelope, there are standard sizes.

| Commercial | Size | Specialty | Size |
|---|---|---|---|
| #6 1/4 | 3 1/2 x 6 | A-2 | 4 3/8 x 5 3/4 |
| #6 3/4 | 3 5/8 x 6 1/2 | A-6 | 4 3/4 x 6 1/2 |
| #7 3/4 | 3 7/8 x 7 1/2 | A-7 | 5 1/4 x 7 1/4 |
| Monarch | 3 7/8 x 7 1/2 | A-8 | 5 1/2 x 8 1/8 |
| #8 5/8 | 3 5/8 x 8 5/8 | A-10 | 6 x 9 1/2 |
| #9 | 3 7/8 x 8 7/8 | Slimline | 3 7/8 x 8 7/8 |
| #10 | 4 1/8 x 9 1/2 | 10 | 4 1/8 x 9 1/2 |
| #11 | 4 1/2 x 10 3/8 | 9 1/2 | 9 x 12 |

*A variety of adhesives works well for affixing fabric accents to scrapbook pages. Two-sided tape designed for use with fabric works well, as do sticky dots, foam squares, and a glue gun.*

## adhering fabric to a page

Attaching fabric to scrapbook pages as the primary background is simple. Using an iron-on or roll-on adhesive assures that the fabric will lay flat and securely on the page. With an iron-on adhesive, it is important to work only with fabrics that can withstand high heat.

First, trim the fabric to the size of the page. You may prefer to allow 1" on all four edges so that the fabric can be pulled to the backside of the page and glued down for a finished look. Begin by covering the backside of the fabric with adhesive. Gently lay fabric on the page and smooth from the center to the edges with your hands. Miter corners and pull excess fabric to backside of page and glue down. You can add as many layers of fabric as you like using this process.

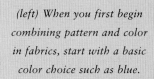

(left) *When you first begin combining pattern and color in fabrics, start with a basic color choice such as blue.*

(right) *A paisley works well because it shares the same color palette as the solid hues.*

*Pink are the flowers of summer's days,*
*Rose is the color of baby's cheeks,*
*Green are the leaves of rose's sweet,*
*Lime is the tang of the lemonade*
*Blue is my love and blue is the sky,*
*Summer so quickly you go by.*

## layering fabric for color & texture

Fabrics bring color and texture to pages in a way that paper cannot. You need look no further than a remnant basket for small pieces of cloth that will make your pages spectacular. Before casting off old clothing or linens, consider what possibilities they may have for your next scrapbooking project.

A simple way to begin working with different fabrics on a page is to choose a color and work with its various hues. For instance, choose a small blue-striped fabric and use a blue plaid in similar tones as its coordinate. As you work more and more with fabrics, you'll become increasingly confident in using bolder combinations.

If you are nervous mixing and matching patterns, begin by looking for a color theme. A paisley fabric with bright pinks and greens can be complemented with a small green plaid and grounded with a soft pink solid.

Fabric pieces can be "hemmed" by securing raw edges turned over with glue. Or, you may want to fray the edges for texture. Ribbon and other trims can cover raw edges and finish a page.

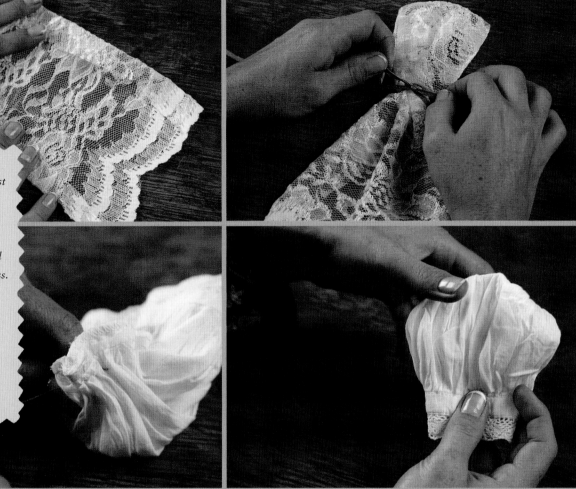

*(top) A piece of pretty lace just happened to fall into the shape of a dress, which was the inspiration for adding a few stitches, some beads, and a bow to make a wedding dress.*

*(bottom) The sleeve from a little girl's white dress was the inspiration for a chef's hat. A piece of thin gingham ribbon and a button finish it off with a little whimsy.*

## creating fabric shapes

When I think of all the ways fabric can be used on scrapbook pages, it reminds me of lying on my back, looking up at the sky, when I was a child. With my imagination soaring, the clouds seemed to be so many different things. Creating shapes with small pieces of fabrics is much the same thing. You don't need to be a seamstress; just a few stitches or hot glue can hold a shape in place. Think of the possibilities:

- A lace cuff can become an apron
- Fabric can be folded into the shape of the miniature paper hats we loved as children
- A square of white linen can become a baby bonnet
- A thin strip of heavy fabric can be frayed on the ends to become a winter scarf
- A piece of netting can become a bridal veil

blue
violets
palette

Rose
palette

WEED PALETTE

## combining colors

Many people tell me they don't know how to combine color and pattern. When working with fabrics for your scrapbook pages, look to nature. Nature is the secret hand that guides my designs and leads my thought process. If you take time to look very closely at a sunset, a mountain, a lake, or an ocean, you will see many, many colors. Some are complementary, others contrasting.

If nature puts certain colors together, it's a safe bet they'll look great on your pages. Look closely at a flower; a pink rose, for instance, has many tones of pink and white, yellow in the center, and of course a green stem and leaves. Even the green has many shades if you study it. All of these colors work together in harmony.

Soon you'll see that fabrics in many different patterns can happily coexist if the colors are from a nature-inspired palette. There is really no great secret, just a natural solution to color.

Sewing is at the heart of our business; even Chris has learned to sew. Using tailoring and sewing techniques on scrapbook pages is a natural for me. Simple things like sewing a thin piece of fabric or ribbon and gathering it as a border adds dimension to a page.

Sewing Chris...

Stitch, tack, needle, craft,
Embroider, embellish, trim and snip,
Thread, bobbin, and here we go —
So many hands make it sew!

# chapter three

# Tailoring Techniques

You don't need to be an experienced seamstress to use sewing and tailoring details on scrapbook pages. If you can sew a straight stitch on a machine, or do the same by hand, you will be successful with the projects in this chapter. A simple sewing machine and a needle and thread are all you need to get started.

A simple straight stitch around the four edges of the page holds the fabric in place. It's much easier to sew through the fabric and the page if you tack the fabric to the paper first. Use an embroidery or needlepoint needle. The pocket is machine stitched to the fabric before it is adhered to the page.

PATTERNS

MCCALL'S
Mommy & Me™
by April Cornell
2102

McCall's
AUGUST FASHION DIGEST and fabric news
7914
(Your) SEWING CENTRE
3 B COMMERCIAL CENTER
TEL. 684-5220
ROXBORO, QUE.          CANADA

PATTERNS
PATTERNS

*The pattern on this page is from one of the very first things I sewed for myself, a corduroy jumper. Years later, when McCall's approached us to design patterns for them, I felt like my sewing had come full circle! The fabric used for the background of this page is sewn using a simple straight stitch with a machine. The edges are allowed to fray so they look raw.*

INSPIRATION

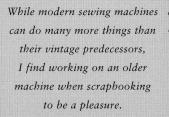

While modern sewing machines
can do many more things than
their vintage predecessors,
I find working on an older
machine when scrapbooking
to be a pleasure.

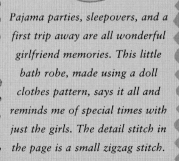

*enduring*

Of all good
things upon
the earth, a
*faithful friend*
is best.

Pajama parties, sleepovers, and a
first trip away are all wonderful
girlfriend memories. This little
bath robe, made using a doll
clothes pattern, says it all and
reminds me of special times with
just the girls. The detail stitch in
the page is a small zigzag stitch.

*memories*

If people concentrated on the really important things in life, there would be a shortage of fishing poles.

Once the fabric was sewn along all four edges of this page with a simple straight machine stitch, the detailing was done with a "freewheeling" stitch. Most machines have a setting for this stitch. If yours does not, you can guide the fabric manually by turning it around and around while feeding it through the machine. The twine is tacked to the page with a manual cross stitch.

A variety of fabric squares are sewn on this page for a patchwork effect. Fraying the edges of fabric is easy. Pull one thread out about ½" in from the raw edge, and then remove all threads from the space it leaves to the edge.

*retreat*

*refresh*

You can approach fabric scrap-booking like a quilt. To do this, assemble and stitch the pieces together into a 12" square, then sew the entire piece to the paper or cardstock. The colors of the tropics, vibrant blues, pinks, and greens, are a perfect background for favorite seaside photos.

My Sincerest Wishes

I want the folks I really care for, to have the ... in this life, therefor... In this greeting I had to in... ...let you know I wished yo...

As You Celebrate 25 Years of Marriage

Smocking is a wonderful sewing technique, but it is not easy, and it is certainly not fast. The background for this page is actually the front of a discarded pillow. It worked perfectly to showcase mementos of our 25th wedding anniversary. The flowers are iron-on appliqués attached with sticky dots.

Our 25th
July 5, 2000
Montreal

Greetings

LOVE

And all Good Wishes

A wide zigzag stitch in a contrasting thread color adds a design element to the page. It works well if you don't use this stitch for every piece of fabric. Note how the pink fabric with the embroidered flower makes a nice mat for the pencil sketch without the stitching.

LET ME PLAY IN THE SUNSHINE; LET ME SING FOR JOY; LET ME GROW IN THE LIGHT; LET ME SPLASH IN THE RAIN, AND REMEMBER THE DAYS OF CHILDHOOD FOREVER.

## happy birthday card

Show friends you care about their birthday with a hand-crafted card. The birthday card is made by cutting one larger square, fraying the edges, and sewing it to the front of a folded piece of cardstock. I like to use watercolor paper for cards. Smaller squares are cut and sewn to the card with a straight stitch sewn diagonally. The greeting is rubber stamped on paper, glued to a strip of hem tape, and attached to the card with decorative paper clips.

## thank you card

Show your gratefulness by folding a piece of card stock in 1/3 of its width on the left and 2/3 of its width on the right side. Cut and fray pieces of fabric to fit each side. Sew fabric onto card. In this version, a slight zigzag stitch was used. For added color, sew a piece of plaid fabric over the right side of the card. Add any scrapbook page embellishments you like. Two brads on either side of the two flaps hold a string that ties the card closed. The greeting is rubber stamped on a small shipping tag and tied to another decorative brad.

You can print greetings on a computer and add them to suit the occasion.

## machine stitches

*(above left)* A zigzag stitch is a basic stitch on a sewing machine, and adds a great design detail to scrapbook pages. Use contrasting color threads for best results. Before you start on the fabric, practice different width and stitch length settings on a remnant piece of fabric.

*(above right)* A free-motion quilting stitch technique is a great way to embellish scrapbook pages. Release the feed dogs on the machine and just guide the page under the needle to make your design.

*(left)* Sewing fabric to paper or card stock is easy. Heavy paper, such as watercolor paper or lightweight poster board, won't rip or tear as lighter papers might. Practice on a small piece of the board and some extra fabric before you work on your page.

### miniature clothing

A miniature bathrobe or any other tiny piece of clothing can make a page a smile-maker. Sewing patterns for doll clothes can be found in the craft section of major sewing pattern books. If you prefer an easier route, try the doll section of a local toy store. Use sticky dots to adhere the clothing to the page so it will not be damaged. Place the robe, or other clothing piece, on the page first, then arrange and affix photos. Embellishments such as buttons go on last, and sticky dots make it easy to affix them too.

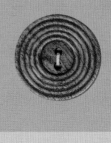

A

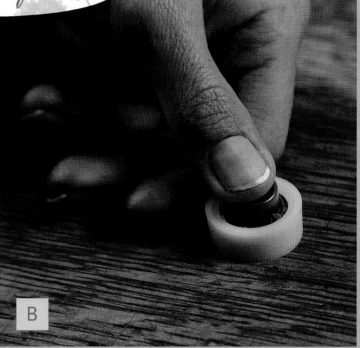

B

C

## c o v e r i n g   a   b u t t o n

Covering your own buttons lets you create the perfect
button to complement your page design. It is very easy
to do. Kits are available in numerous button sizes at fabric
stores. Begin by cutting a circle of fabric about ½" larger
in circumference than the button you are covering. (A) Fold
the edges of the fabric over the metal teeth of the button
top. (B) Place the button top inside the plastic holder
provided in the kit. Place the metal back of the button
in place and, using the implement provided in the kit, bear
down until the back snaps into place. (C) The result is an
inexpensive custom button to decorate your page.

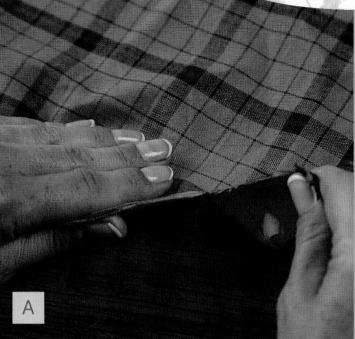

A

B

C

## fraying fabric

To fray the edges of fabric, begin by working with the grain. Determine the grain by making a small cut in the edge of the fabric and testing to see if it will tear. If it tears easily, you are working with the grain. (A) Tear the two edges of the fabric that go with the grain. Depending on the fabric, you may have to use scissors to cut the other two sides. (B) Choose a thread about $1/2$" from each edge and pull it out. (C) Work from the space the missing thread creates and remove all the threads to the edge of the fabric.

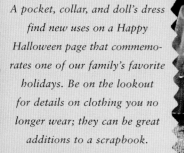

*A pocket, collar, and doll's dress find new uses on a Happy Halloween page that commemorates one of our family's favorite holidays. Be on the lookout for details on clothing you no longer wear; they can be great additions to a scrapbook.*

# chapter four

# Clever Clothing Uses

So often a favorite memory includes what we or someone else was wearing at the time. Yet, as fashion comes and goes or a stain or two takes its toll on a favorite garment, you may find that a piece of clothing has not been out of the closet in years. Why not make a favorite frock part of a special page? In this chapter, we take a look at countless uses for pieces of clothing.

Forcing bulbs in a glass jar gives spring to winter
Painting on a quiet day gives interest to my life
I study my tulip bulb and its shapely jar in reflected water
Feeling its energy and developing blooms;
through my pencil and brush I feel united with the
hope of spring...tulip bulb in winter.

The four points of a collar,
a placket with button loops, and
a pocket of a voile dress make
this page a floral treat to
celebrate the coming of spring.
Beads strung on embroidery
thread are woven through the
button loops and yellow buds
adorn a trim that accents the
page. One photo of sweet blue
flowers is pinned to a fabric
beverage coaster.

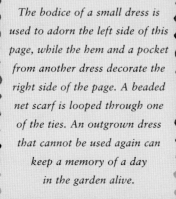

Chris and I share flowers in the garden

April Cornell for Cornell Trading

save the flowers in a pocket!

... my flowers, share my flowers, save the flowers in a pocket!

The bodice of a small dress is used to adorn the left side of this page, while the hem and a pocket from another dress decorate the right side of the page. A beaded net scarf is looped through one of the ties. An outgrown dress that cannot be used again can keep a memory of a day in the garden alive.

## project

### the business of memories

Even though most business contacts end up in a computer database, I still like to hold onto attractive business cards of the interesting people I meet. A good business card expresses some of its owner's personality, and I find I like holding onto it. You may feel the same way about a collection of cards from favorite restaurants or shops.

Fabric can easily be made into an attractive business card holder you can either carry in your purse or tuck in a drawer. Cut two rectangular pieces of fabric 6" wide and 8" high using pinking shears. With the fabrics back to back, iron the two pieces together using fusible interfacing. Once the fabrics have cooled, gently fold the sides of the top edges together to find the middle point. Using pinking shears, cut at an angle on either side to create a pointed "flap." Fold the rectangle together 2" from the top. Glue the sides together with fabric glue. Turn the flap down, and glue in place. Using a hot glue gun, affix a decorative button.

Gabrielle, Vivian and Rachel
The Cornell girls in summer party blue

One of the very first fashion
shoots we did was of three girls
in blue summer party dresses.
It was a benchmark for us and
a very exciting time. Two small
dresses from the Cornelloki dolls
are the perfect way for me to
remember this highlight. Vintage
business cards from our early
days are printed on vellum and
attached to the page using
upholstery pins. The hibiscus
flowers were cut from cotton
fabric and ironed onto the page.

Flower picking...
...Lavender in my pocket...
Singing birds...
...Happy day!

A piece of embroidery from the
bodice of a blouse is framed
with the floral hem of a dress.
The embroidered ecru corners
are collars. A pocket holds dried
lavender from one of my walks.

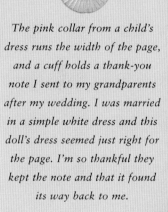

The pink collar from a child's dress runs the width of the page, and a cuff holds a thank-you note I sent to my grandparents after my wedding. I was married in a simple white dress and this doll's dress seemed just right for the page. I'm so thankful they kept the note and that it found its way back to me.

A velvet toddler coat makes me think of a gardening jacket and the joy of spending spring days in the garden. If you don't want to damage a piece of children's clothing, you can turn the extra parts onto the reverse side of the page and pin it. It is a good idea to use cardboard for this type of page because it is much sturdier.

A favorite velvet jacket in hues of violet and blue, Easter memories, seeds, chicks and eggs for a few.

SWISS GIANT MIXED COLORS
PANSY

The placket, hem ruffle, and pocket from a torn dress make this page a fun hodge podge of some of my favorite things. An inexpensive wood frame is covered with fabric using spray adhesive.

Black-eyed Susans shared the garden and through the pretty window of my shed, I watched the single pear grow so beautifully...

My pear tree bore a single fruit its first year....

May 25/95
Having the ... and ...
jittery about H... with gued
Reader- Neriam flight to t
scheduled to ... in ... Belie-
Cochin this ... the ... Needless
Kaur + Tamanni's ... almost 10 am
to say little & tiny ones
way late a Sharma in
so the ... had coffee
Finally was a peaceful
Cochin chamel city
went ... lew Town
+ bentris at

## project

### clothed in memories album

Making a custom photo album from scratch is a project for the brave, but if you start with a store-bought version there are countless things you can do to it to make it special. For this fun album, start with a 12" x 12" spiral-bound photo album. To create the image, place a favorite piece of clothing, in this case a wool jacket, on a color photocopier loaded with photograph paper. Trim the top of the image and mount onto piece of red cardstock. Bring the jacket to life by gluing coordinating buttons and a pocket to the image. Mount the cardstock on the front of the album using liquid archival glue.

Working with several coordinating fabrics and ribbons torn or cut into 6" strips, tie them around the spiral binding. The actual pocket from a garment adds dimension. Tuck a special letter or a piece of treasured memorabilia in the pocket as a happy reminder.

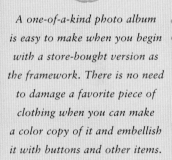

A one-of-a-kind photo album is easy to make when you begin with a store-bought version as the framework. There is no need to damage a favorite piece of clothing when you can make a color copy of it and embellish it with buttons and other items.

Collars can be used as corners, borders, flaps, or to hold collectibles on a page.

Hems can be used as borders or frames on a page.

Cuffs can be used as simple adornments, pockets, or cut into whimsical shapes.

Pockets, more than any other
clothing detail, are perfect
for their intended use—
to hold things!

Plackets make good frames,
borders, finished edges,
and places to tuck
photos and cards.

Ruffles can be used to give
a page dimension. They are
perfect for borders, corners,
and to frame something
you want to be a focal
point on the page.

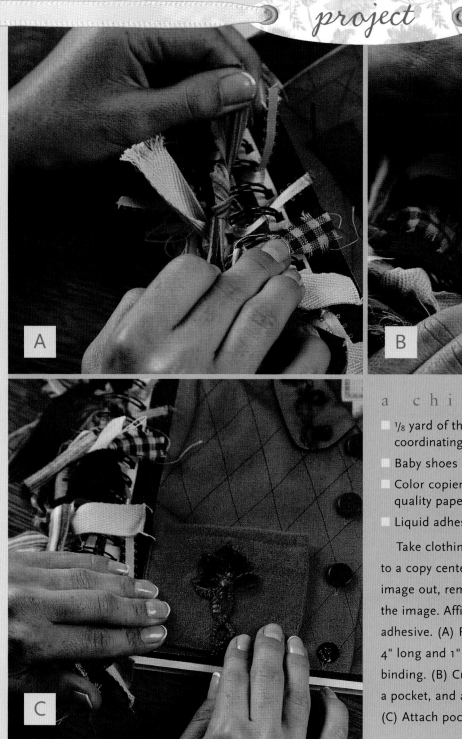

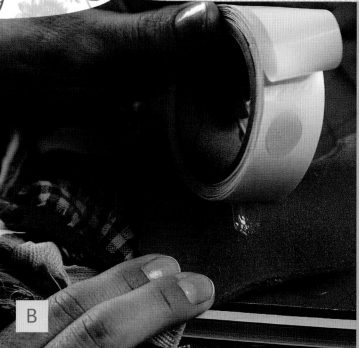

## a child's album

- 1/8 yard of three coordinating cotton fabrics
- Baby shoes
- Color copier and photo quality paper
- Liquid adhesive
- Mounting tape
- Purchased photo album
- Scissors
- Special piece of children's clothing
- Twine

Take clothing you want to feature on an album cover to a copy center and color copy to scale of album. Cut image out, removing any parts of the paper that is not the image. Affix to the front of the album using liquid adhesive. (A) Rip coordinating cotton fabrics into strips 4" long and 1" wide. Tie and knot fabric strips to spiral binding. (B) Cut a piece of the actual clothing, in this case a pocket, and adhere large sticky dots to the back. (C) Attach pocket to page using light pressure.

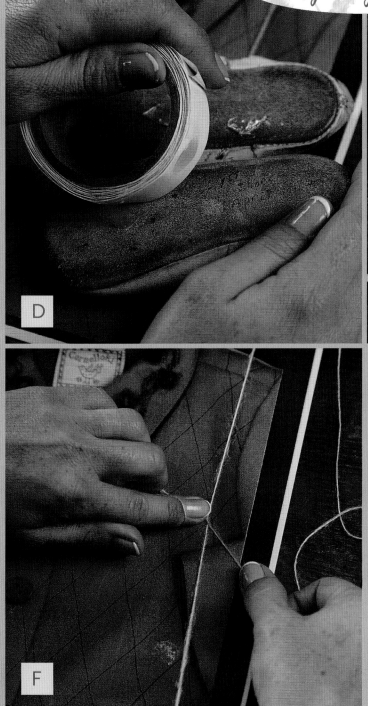

D

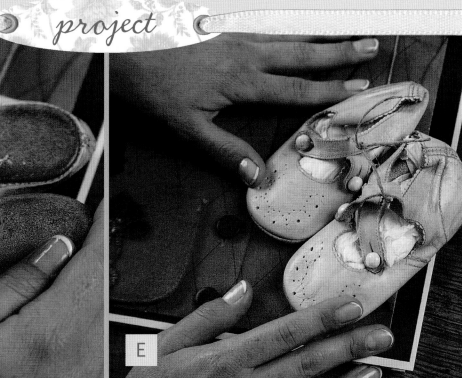

E

F

(D and E) Repeat steps B and C for any other items, such as baby shoes, you would like to include. (F) Album can be tied closed using a piece of twine. Affix the twine to the back cover of the album with a decorative sticker so that it is not separated from the album when it is opened.

Rather than consign never-worn jewelry, broken pieces, or an orphan earring, use them to make your scrapbook pages special. Here, turquoise beads bring tropical blue waters to life and remind me of many happy days along the water—whether a lake in Vermont or Quebec or the warm waters of the Caymans.

Tranquil Waters

# chapter five

# Dazzling Jewels

Single earrings without a mate, broken necklaces, and unworn souvenir beads seem to languish in a drawer. They can make rich embellishments to your pages, so find a special place to collect them and begin using each piece to bring dazzle to your already sparkling memories.

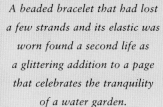

A beaded bracelet that had lost a few strands and its elastic was worn found a second life as a glittering addition to a page that celebrates the tranquility of a water garden.

A Few of My Favorite Things!

A little bird told me ~

Cameron along a Dutch canal ~

Years later Leandra in a field ~

A silver bracelet of semi-precious teardrop stones dresses up the corner of this page. The beaded bracelet had ended up like several others, broken and fragile, but it looks wonderful on a page with memories of two special children.

Any page that marks a special wedding deserves extra special treatment. It was the perfect place for two unused pendants, one in the shape of a heart. Inexpensive faux pearls are glued around the border of the page.

*Barbara Weds!*

*I Do*

*now and forever*

## frame the day

A simple wood frame becomes a precious gift when it is adorned with lovely jewelry pieces. To begin, sand a wood frame and paint it with flat pink paint. Once the paint has completely dried, stencil or write words or a phrase along the bottom of the frame. Embellish the frame with vintage trims and ribbon, bits of handmade papers, and other details such as crochet flowers, fanciful trims, and glass beads. An earring without a mate and a pendant are the crowning touch of this frame. Surely you have a few other pieces you could use too.

The image on this page is done using the same technique for making a color print of a garment described on page 82. A necklace, loosely tacked to the bottom of the page, complements the rich brocade of the silk in the jacket.

remember this

**When You're Sick**

To my number two son Lee,
It's with you I'd like to be,
... your head, and give you tea,
... ts of honey from a bee!

... d your stories in your bed,
... a nap and rest your head,
... reams of popsicles instead
... the morning time - your throat will
be extra fine!

... love and kisses
Mom & Dad.

A.H.    4/b-
9643632

Cornell Trading Ltd.

Lee Cornell
(please deliver today!)

Tues.
APRIL 16 '91

LOVE

*Running the necklace down the
right side of a page dedicated to
my son, Lee, reminds me of the
special gifts from my boys when
they were young. You might
have a few small treasures that
were preschool crafts, presented
so proudly to you by little hands.
A scrapbook page is the perfect
showcase for these special jewels
along with a photo of the
young artist.*

The Nutcracker was a family
tradition for many years. The
boys danced a variety of parts
including the mouse and the
prince. Since the theater is a
regular showcase for ladies in
their jewels, I think the little
mouse deserves a gem or two.

Look out Rudolf Nu...

The Nutcracker

Cameron
Lee
Grandpa

The Cornells became such a fixture in The Nutcracker that their grandfather even got into the act one year. What wonderful memories! A necklace runs across the center of the page and is held in place by gold and red braiding attached with a hot glue gun.

Our camp at Bark Lake is truly
a gem. The pendants here were
samples used while designing
a particular season's line.
I love the idea of using jewels
altogether. Single earrings may
never find their mates, so for
now they look quite nice along-
side photos taken at the lake.

memories

enjoy

remember

A pretty paper box is the perfect gathering place for jewelry pieces that can be used on scrapbook pages. You are much more apt to use recycled jewelry if it is easily accessible while you are working on your scrapbooks. Have fun creating a special gem of a box to display in your craft area.

A

B

C

D

a treasure box

Decoupage medium

Dimensional stickers

Foam brush

Glass beads
  to complement color
  of silk flowers

Glue gun

Jewelry embellishments

Paper cutouts

Round kraft paper box

Silk flowers

Yellow craft paint

Paint a cardboard round box yellow using craft paint and foam brush. (A) Using paper cutouts you have chosen, adhere to the box using the decoupage medium applied with a foam brush. You may choose to trim paper to be about 1/2" smaller than bottom side of the box so some of the yellow shows. (B) Use a hot glue gun to affix silk flowers to the sides of the box top. (C) Add more flowers, gluing glass beads to the centers. Add dimensional stickers. (D) Choose a piece of jewelry to be the crowning touch on the lid.

*(top left)* Necklaces can be used as borders, to frame a favorite photo, or to hang on a page as a focal point. They can be attached to a page with sewn loops, glue, or two-sided tape.

*(bottom left)* Fanciful pins and brooches add whimsy to a page and can be used in a variety of ways, including animating a fashion statement. Pin them through the page to secure.

*(top right)* Bracelets can adorn the corner of a page, crown a photo, or embellish an empty spot on a page. Adhere the same way you would a necklace.

*(bottom right)* Earrings make beautiful embellishments, especially if they are designed for pierced ears. Use a sharp tool to pierce a small hole through the page and insert the earring(s). Embellishing scrapbook pages is a wonderful use for orphan earrings.

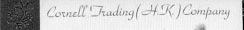

Cornell Trading (H.K.) Company

**James Kwan**
General Manager
(China Region)

Room 1201, 12/F., Max Trade Centre,
23 Luk Hop Street, San Po Kong, Kowloon, Hong Kong.
Tel.: (852) 2814 9449   E-mail: cornell@hknet.com   Fax: (852) 2580 1671

*We seem to collect all kinds of objects when we travel. Foreign coins and currency are obvious items, and we have the inevitable postcards. The ivory pieces tucked into the pocket are bookmarks given to me by the man who runs our Hong Kong office. The trim features small coins, and is the perfect addition to the page.*

HONG KONG                    香港

# Bits and Pieces

Wherever we travel, we always seem to gather all sorts of small trinkets. When I sift through my photos and the memorabilia I have saved there always seems to be some small object falling onto the floor. Scrapbook pages are a wonderful place to showcase memorabilia that adds special interest that photos may not. I hope you find some inspiration on these pages to gather as you go.

Autumn
retreat

Often a friend will send a thank you or a special thought on a little note. I hate to discard these, so I tuck them into a pocket on a page. I am always gathering leaves, especially when we are at Bark Lake, and what better way to bring more than just the sense of sight to preserving memories?

I encourage others to carry
a gathering bag on their nature
walks. It is the perfect way to
collect autumn leaves, pods,
ferns, and other gifts of nature.
Because fallen leaves can become
very brittle, display a page like
this out of a book so that it will
not be damaged by rubbing
against other pages.

The trees around the camp at Bark Lake shed the most wonderful white bark. It flattens fairly easily and can be used for paintings, written verses, and as a background accent on a page. Because of the properties of bark, use copies of anything you place on the page; it is not archival and you can't be sure what it will do to images over time.

[FOREVERFRIENDS]

Crocheted cherries were part of a collection of embellishments we were reviewing for one of our seasonal lines. They seemed like the perfect addition to the blackbird page. The blackbird is ironed onto the page using fusible webbing.

Mother

SENSATION MIX

COSMOS

NET WT
650 mg

MENT

They say that grandmothers are
antique little girls, so I thought
it was sweet to use a fabric doll
on the same page as a photo
of my mother. The back of the
doll was opened up and about
half of her stuffing was removed
so that she looked a little more
comfortable on the page.

The days of the boys as babies were short, but the memories are sweet. This little bunny (with half of his stuffing removed too) reminds me of play days and kisses from baby boys in blue.

Bunny
Love in Blue
Sweet Baby Boy

One of the boys drew a picture of a whale on this puzzle, probably when we were in the Caymans. Rather than tuck it into a box somewhere it gets a special spot on a page. You can make your own puzzle and arrange the pieces together on a page to reveal a message or to tell a story.

Life all together... fits

Sometimes cards, brochures, and papers picked up on travels tell it all and no descriptions are necessary.

# Tibet Festival

*Programs from events can be mounted on a page along with a photo and other decorative details to tell a story. Don't glue the program shut; leave it open so that you and others can read through it and reminisce.*

Support Conservation, Support BNHS

**Friends of**
BNHS

Visit us at www.bnhs.org

It looks as if Kelly was not having as good a time as the rest of us! Small works by local artisans, such as the wooden art elephant, work well on scrapbook pages. Stickers and buttons from groups or events are also good keepsakes for pages.

Small lengths of trim with chunky beads add detail to a page showcasing highlights of our Eastern travels. Painted wood picture frames are available at craft stores and can be easily distressed by painting and then sanding with coarse sandpaper.

*Rich brocade fabric on the page reflects the native dress we are wearing in the photos. Coins appear to be adhered to the page strung on metallic ribbon. They are actually affixed using double-stick foam squares with the ribbon placed between the coins and the fabric pocket.*

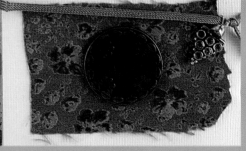

*If something is beautiful, I never throw it out. The lid of a box covered with vintage hand-screened wallpaper is a treasure because of the image of a cardinal. Long after the box became tattered, the lid was kept and now is a perfect adornment for a winter birding page.*

when it's cold outside

bundle up

cheers!

Stay Warm

A child's mitten, its mate long lost, is delightful decoration that recalls a winter snowball fight. The three photos at the top of the page are matted on black paper, holes punched on the inside edges and tied together with small pieces of fabric.

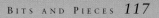

If you kept scrapbooks in your younger years, you may find, as I did, that they are falling apart and need to be redone. I found the insignia from my school drama days and a cartoon I clipped as a teenager among the aging pages. Cartoons are a wonderful way to capture how you were feeling or what amused you at different stages of your life.

RIVERDALE DRAMA
T. I. O. B. E.

NO... I DON'T WANT TO WAKE UP ONE MORNING, MIDDLE-AGED AND REALIZE I WASN'T EVEN A HAS-BEEN, DADDY!

The Protestant School Commissioners
for the Municipality of St. Laurent

Protestant School Board
of Greater Montreal

HIGH SCHOOL
GRADES VIII AND I
RIVERDALE HIGH
5059 WOODLAND
PIERREFONDS,

REPORT O

April Milne

Mr.

TO PARENTS OR GUARD

Since this report is issued for the information of
parents, they are requested to examine it carefully
and to acknowledge its receipt by signing in the
space provided for that purpose.

Unsatisfactory progress or any irregularity in the
report should be made a matter of immediate
inquiry by the parent concerned who may then
arrange for a conference with the principal.

*The program from my high
school commencement, my
student identification card, as
well as photo booth candid shots
tell a story without captions.
A favorite ring from my teenage
years is tied to the page with
the same trim that keeps the
program neatly closed.*

SEMPER NOSTRUM OPTIMUM

R H S

April Milne
is a member of

Riverdale High School
Students' Association

A. Kearns
President

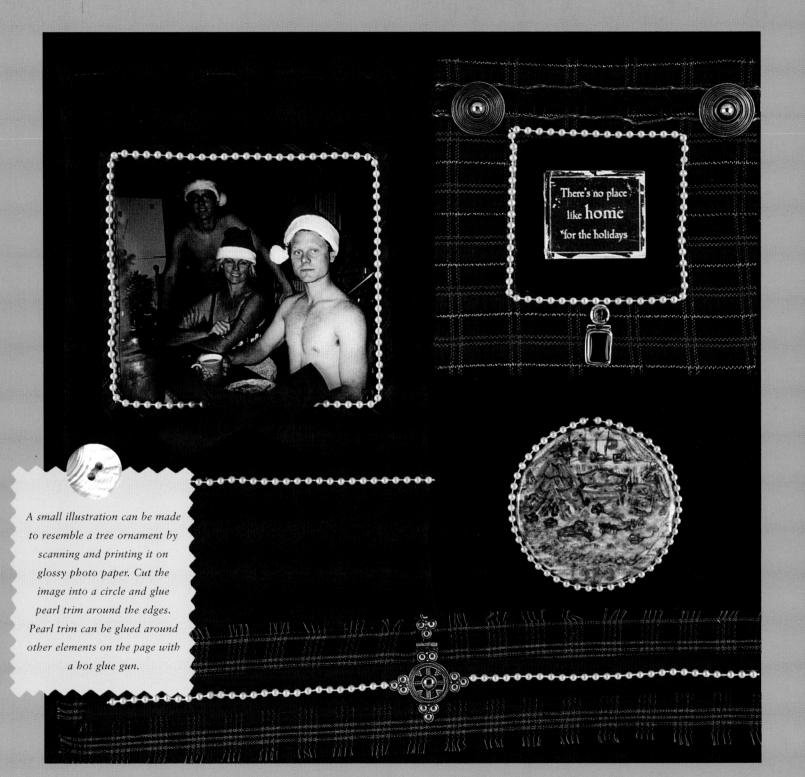

There's no place like **home** for the holidays

A small illustration can be made to resemble a tree ornament by scanning and printing it on glossy photo paper. Cut the image into a circle and glue pearl trim around the edges. Pearl trim can be glued around other elements on the page with a hot glue gun.

*A handkerchief would have been tucked into the pocketbook of my aunties, and the pearl buttons are just like ones that adorned their dresses. The skeleton key reminds me of the one that opened the front door back home. These objects bring back warm memories of the ladies in my life.*

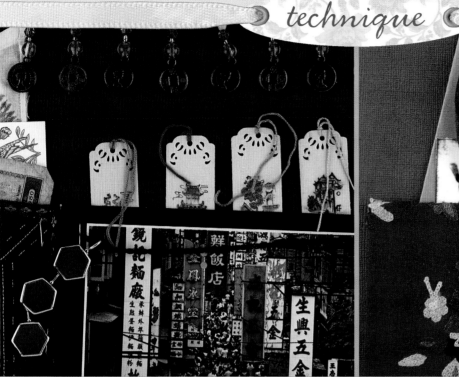

## found objects on pages

*(above left)* Similar items can be grouped on a page by stringing them together with embroidery thread or thin ribbon.

*(above right)* Dried leaves and flowers can be tucked into pockets on a page. The best way to dry them is to place them between the pages of a telephone book and stack several heavy books on top. Allow about a month to dry.

*(left)* Tree bark can be wonderful to work with in scrapbooking or journaling. Only work with bark that has fallen from the tree or is completely peeled away from the trunk. You can kill a tree removing its bark. Lay the bark flat and press it under books the same way you would leaves or flowers. If the bark is brittle, soak it in water before pressing it flat.

## thoughtful touches

*(above left)* Cartoons and newspaper comics capture what we thought was amusing at a particular point in our lives. I saved this cartoon when I was a teenager. It appears I never thought I'd be middle-aged. The joke was on me!

*(above right)* A program or card can be neatly held closed when tied with a ribbon. Consider including a keepsake such as a favorite ring.

*(left)* A nostalgic item added to a page does not need to be vintage or expensive. A handkerchief from the bridal section of a craft store is embellished with a faux stick pin designed for scrapbook pages.

A dear lady I met in a nursing home in India peers out from a frame made of an embroidered fabric border with small mirror disks. Bold trims and ribbons make wonderful frames. Metallic ribbon makes a big impact and brings the richness of India alive.

# chapter seven

# Ribbons, Trims, and Doodads

Pages rich in detail are much more interesting than those that are not. Ribbons, trims, and other embellishments are easy to use and make the difference between blah and aah. Keep a collection of short lengths of trims and ribbons in a special spot with your scrapbooking materials. I buy a yard or two of beautiful trim whenever I see it. It is easier to create exceptional pages when I already have supplies on hand. In this chapter, you will learn to use ribbons, trims, buttons, and milliners flowers in wonderful ways.

Stretch lace divides the page into quadrants, essentially creating four mini-pages. A straw milliner's flower, used on hats, can be purchased online. A small piece of ribbon flower trim accents the top right side of the page.

One crazy kindergartner posing for the camera!

Two friends in a boat
Water birding with Helene in India

Two friends with a goat
Kelly and cousin Gala in British Columbia

*Friends*

We use personalized ribbon as hanger loops in our clothing line. You can order ribbon with your name, your family's name, or a message through Internet web sites or party supply stores. It's fairly inexpensive, and is a wonderful way to make pages extra special.

## project

### beautiful button jar

Buttons can become a collecting obsession, and having plenty on hand means you always have the perfect final details for a page. You'll be inspired to use buttons if you can see your collection. Small glass containers that look like mason jars are inexpensive and can be found at a craft or import store. Cut a small, round piece of fabric the size of the top of the jar, and use a liquid laminate to adhere it to the top of the jar. Once the fabric is dry, embellish the jar with buttons, beaded trims, and ribbons. Use a hot glue gun to affix trims and ribbons.

Small shell buttons come in numerous shapes and sizes and add delightful details. Small round buttons can be used as berries, a star is a yuletide accent, and a pearly leaf suggests a holly bush. If you keep a button jar filled with possibilities, you'll find countless uses for the little gems.

Crochet flower trim in bright
green and blue lends a fanciful
air to a tropical page. The trim
is new, but has a vintage flair.
To encase a photo, cut a frame
from cardboard, using a crafting
knife. Use a spray adhesive, and
then lay the fabric over it, with
the wrong side facing down
toward the board. Use the knife
to cut the fabric from the center
of the frame, leaving a 1" allow-
ance. Miter corners and adhere
raw edges of fabric to backside
of the frame and glue in place.

**CORN**

NK LAWN & GARDEN CO.

·SWEET·

Net Wt. .75 OZ

BUTTER & SUGAR HYBRID

strawberries mmm

*Summer*

The edges of a summery page are finished with a multi-colored loop trim affixed to the page with straight pins. The trim is elastic, which makes it easy to work with. The frame is from the April Cornell line, and embellished with ribbon trim and the simple word "Summer."

FRom: Olivia

To ARil

*As Olivia sees me at 50!*

One of the most beautiful
birthday gifts I have received
is a portrait of me by my
niece, Olivia. The picture is
framed in signature ribbon,
and the borders of the page
are adorned with large buttons
and whimsical ribbons.

April Cornell®  April Cornell®  April Cornell®  April Cornell®

April Cornell®  April Cornell®  April Cornell®  April Corn

Turning 50 was pure fun thanks to a surprise party my family threw for me. Wired beads frame my delighted expression with the evening's festivities—they made me Queen for a Day! Photos don't all have to be from the same occasion; I included the shot of me with the hula hoop because it fit the spirit.

The Boreal woods surrounding Bark Lake have inspired much of my design work. I am especially intrigued by the mushrooms that grow there. When designing a page about a special place, include not only the people and events, but also what nature was like at the time. Whether it is fallen leaves or blooming buds, it's all part of the memory.

My mother has always been my cheerleader and a devoted mentor to my creative interests. Not only does she hold a special place in my heart, but in my scrapbook as well. Trim frames her nurse's portrait and runs down the sides of the page. A teacup appliqué holds the treasure of Cape Breton, Nova Scotia roses.

My mother so pretty, my mother so young...
Her nurse's cap proud worn over dark waving hair,
Curls on crisp white of her uniform.
Duty and beauty combined in a true Nova Scotia girl.
Uncle and auntie join the sweet, salty song,
Cape Breton roses your scent is strong – long.

The colors of a tropical sunset inspired a drawing by one of the boys, and it in turn inspired the selection of fabrics and ribbon on a page. A vivid stripe in the foreground reflects the many colors of the sun. Brilliant wired French ribbon is used on opposite corners.

Trims and velvet ribbons bring color and dimension to one of the first portraits I did as an art student. Patterns and textures mix well because they match the color palette of the floral fabric used as a background.

*Oil portrait of a model by me*
*—Roxboro 1967*

*technique*

### details, details...

*(above left)* Trims make ideal frames for photographs, special papers, and keepsakes. Use a glue gun to adhere trim. Mitered corners look best.

*(above right)* Trims make wonderful borders on scrapbook pages too. A 48" piece of trim or ribbon will cover all edges of a 12" x 12" scrapbook page. Just to be safe, buy 1½ yards, and keep it for just the right page.

*(left)* Whether it is store bought or homemade, a small frame is a great dimensional element for a scrapbook page.

L O V E

## ...and more details

(above left) Appliqués, especially flowers, make a page elegant and lend a vintage hand-sewn feel to a page. Appliqués can be salvaged from used clothing or purchased at major fabric stores.

(above right) It is hard to discard pretty greeting cards. Often, they contain images and words that sum up a feeling or event.

(left) The border of a fringed scarf makes a natural texture trim for a page.

# stores

## UNITED STATES

### ALABAMA

**Birmingham**
The Summit
(205) 970-1660

### ARIZONA

**Scottsdale**
Kierland Commons
(480) 607-7790

**Tucson**
La Encantada
(520) 615-9869

### CALIFORNIA

**Berkeley**
1774 Fourth Street
(510) 527-0715

**Corte Madera**
Village at Corte Madera
(415) 924-5880

**La Jolla**
1000 Prospect Avenue
(858) 454-1980

**Newport Beach**
Fashion Island
Shopping Center
(949) 721-9061

**Palm Desert**
The Gardens on El Paseo
(760) 341-8372

**Pasadena**
340 East Colorado Blvd.
(626) 440-7253

**Sacramento**
Arden Fair Mall
(916) 925-5940

**San Diego**
Fashion Valley Center
(619) 298-8482

**Santa Barbara**
301 Paseo Nuevo
(805) 899-4689

**Santa Clara**
Valley Fair Mall
(408) 261-9970

**Walnut Creek**
1180 Broadway Plaza
(925) 939-2437

### COLORADO

**Boulder**
1123 Pearl Street
(303) 442-3723

**Broomfield**
Flat Iron Crossing
(303) 439-2179

**Denver**
Cherry Creek
Shopping Center
(303) 316-9898

### CONNECTICUT

**Danbury**
Danbury Fair Mall
(203) 791-1137

**Farmington**
West Farms Mall
(860) 521-1923

**Greenwich**
92 Greenwich Avenue
(203) 661-3563

### FLORIDA

**Miami**
The Falls Shopping Center
(305) 254-2204

**Palm Beach**
The Gardens of the
Palm Beaches
(561) 625-6979

**Tampa**
Old Hyde Park Village
(813) 251-3019

### GEORGIA

**Atlanta**
Lenox Square Mall
(404) 812-1722

Perimeter Mall
(770) 671-0722

**Augusta**
Augusta Mall
(770) 447-8021

**Norcross**
The Forum
Shopping Center
(770) 447-8021

### ILLINOIS

**Deer Park**
20530 N. Rand Road
(847) 540-5909

**Geneva**
Geneva Commons
(630) 845-0074

**Northbrook**
Northbrook Court
(847) 564-8570

**Oakbrook**
Oakbrook Center
(630) 574-3066

### INDIANA

**Indianapolis**
Keystone Fashion Mall West
(317) 569-9289

### MARYLAND

**Annapolis**
16 Marketspace
(410) 263-4532

**Baltimore**
The Gallery at Harbor Place
(410) 234-0050

Village at Cross Keys
(410) 433-7266

**Hagerstown**
Hagerstown Prime Outlets
(301) 790-1313

**Towson**
Towson Town Center
(410) 823-0833

### MASSACHUSETTS

**Boston**
Faneuil Hall Marketplace
(617) 248-0280

**Cambridge**
43 Brattle Street
(617) 661-8910

**Newton**
The Mall at Chestnut Hill
(617) 965-1126

**Wrentham**
Wrentham Premium Outlets
(508) 384-9538

### MICHIGAN

**Lansing**
Eastwood Towne Center
(517) 485-7940

**Troy**
Somerset Collection North
(248) 816-9660

### MINNESOTA

**Edina**
The Galleria Mall
(952) 836-0830

### MISSOURI

**Kansas City**
Country Club Plaza
(816) 960-0333

**St. Louis**
Saint Louis Galleria
(314) 725-0120

### NEW HAMPSHIRE

**North Conway**
Settlers' Green
(603) 356-0820

### NEW JERSEY

**Bridgewater**
Bridgewater Commons
(908) 218-9699

**Princeton**
51 Palmer Square West
(609) 921-3559

**Short Hills**
The Mall at Short Hills
(973) 258-0660

**Shrewsbury**
The Grove at Shrewsbury
(732) 758-0066

### NEW YORK

**Central Valley**
Woodbury Common
(845) 928-4885

**Ithaca**
The Commons
(607) 277-5515

**New York**
487 Columbus Avenue
(212) 799-4342

**Waterloo**
Waterloo Premium Outlets
(315) 539-0140

### NORTH CAROLINA

**Raleigh**
Crabtree Valley Mall
(919) 781-7817

Triangle Town Center
(919) 792-2820

### OHIO

**Cincinnati**
Kenwood Town Centre
(513) 936-8819

Lyndhurst
Legacy Village
(216) 382-7190

**OREGON**

Eugene
*Maggie Rhodes*
248 E. 5th Avenue
(541) 686-3329

Portland
Pioneer Place
(503) 222-2171

**PENNSYLVANIA**

Ardmore
Suburban Square
(610) 642-9540

King of Prussia
Court of King of Prussia
(610) 265-0317

Philadelphia
The Shops at Liberty Place
(215) 981-0350

**SOUTH CAROLINA**

Charleston
Charleston Place
(843) 805-7000

Greenville
Greenville Mall
(864) 234-9667

**TENNESSEE**

Memphis
Oak Court Mall
(901) 767-9110

**TEXAS**

Austin
The Arboretum
(512) 345-9908

Dallas
1014 North Park Center
(214) 750-8338

Houston
River Oaks Shopping Center
(713) 520-0426

Plano
The Shops at Willow Bend
(972) 202-5536

**VERMONT**

Burlington
87 Church Street
(802) 862-8211

**VIRGINIA**

Arlington
Fashion Centre
at Pentagon City
(703) 415-2290

Charlottesville
Barracks Road
Shopping Center
(434) 295-9121

McLean
Tysons Corner Center
(703) 448-6972

Norfolk
MacArthur Center
(757) 625-5804

Richmond
Stony Point Fashion Park
(804) 330-7053

**WASHINGTON**

Bellevue
215 Bellevue Square
(425) 455-9818

Redmond
*Maggie Rhodes*
16527 NE 74th Street
(425) 885-0185

Seattle
West Lake Center
(206) 749-9658

**WASHINGTON D.C.**

Georgetown
3278 M Street NW
(202) 625-7887

**WISCONSIN**

Wauwatosa
Mayfair
(414) 476-8776

# CANADA

**ALBERTA**

Banff
Cascade Plaza
(403) 760-3974

Calgary
South Centre Mall
(403) 271-3536

Scotia Centre
(403) 263-5545

Edmonton
W. Edmonton Mall
(780) 481-2038

Southgate Mall
(780) 437-9406

**BRITISH COLUMBIA**

Vancouver
2956 Granville Street
(604) 731-8343

Victoria
Eaton Centre
(250) 384-6343

West Vancouver
Park Royal North
Shopping Centre
(604) 926-3250

**NOVA SCOTIA**

Bedford
Sunnyside Mall
(902) 835-0078

Halifax
Park Lane Mall
(902) 423-1844

**ONTARIO**

Burlington
Mapleview Mall
(905) 639-6489

Hamilton
Jackson Square
(905) 528-3270

Kingston
208 Princess Street
(613) 544-0905

London
White Oaks Mall
(519) 680-7412

Newmarket
Upper Canada Mall
(905) 836-9158

Ottawa
763 Bank Street
(613) 233-0412

Sarnia
136 Front Street North
(519) 383-1477

Stratford
87 Ontario Street
(519) 273-6617

Toronto
346 Queen Street West
(416) 979-8140

2619 Yonge Street
(416) 482-8480

2264 Bloor Street West
(416) 760-7592

**PRINCE EDWARD
ISLAND**

Charlottetown
Confederation Court Mall
(902) 569-5716

**QUEBEC**

Hudson
425 rue Principale
(450) 458-1717

Laval
Carrefour Laval
(450) 973-9961

Montréal
108 Gallery Square
(514) 846-1091

3941 rue St-Denis
(514) 842-7693

Place Montréal Trust
(514) 847-5307

Mt-Tremblant
118 ch. Kandahar
(819) 681-6363

Outremont
1051 rue Laurier Ouest
(514) 273-9700

Pte-Claire
Fairview
(514) 426-1616

Ste-Foy
Place de la Cité
(418) 651-1305

Vieux-Quebec
1150 rue St-Jean
(418) 692-0398

Westmount
1353 Avenue Greene
(514) 935-4361

# acknowledgments

**Page Designers:**
April Cornell
Sherri Allsman
Jayne Cosh
Paige Hill
Susan Novak
Stacie Potokar

**Project Designers:**
Paige Hill
Eileen Paulin
Stacie Potokar

**Photographers:**
Ryne Hazen / *pages and projects*
Mick Hales / *Bark Lake*
Courtney Platt / *The Caymans*

**Photo Stylist:**
Rebecca Ittner

**Project Manager:**
Jayne Cosh

**Graphic Design:**
Deborah Kehoe,
*Kehoe + Kehoe Design Associates, Inc.*
Carolyn Brown
Lynn Lantz

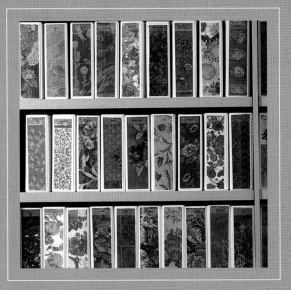

# metric conversion charts

| inches to millimeters and centimeters | | | | | | | | yards to meters | | | | | | | | | | |
|---|---|---|---|---|---|---|---|---|---|---|---|---|---|---|---|---|---|---|
| inches | mm | cm | inches | cm | inches | cm | yards | meters | yards | meters | yards | meters | yards | meters | yards | meters |
| $\frac{1}{8}$ | 3 | 0.3 | 9 | 22.9 | 30 | 76.2 | $\frac{1}{8}$ | 0.11 | $2\frac{1}{8}$ | 1.94 | $4\frac{1}{8}$ | 3.77 | $6\frac{1}{8}$ | 5.60 | $8\frac{1}{8}$ | 7.43 |
| $\frac{1}{4}$ | 6 | 0.6 | 10 | 25.4 | 31 | 78.7 | $\frac{1}{8}$ | 0.11 | $2\frac{1}{8}$ | 1.94 | $4\frac{1}{8}$ | 3.77 | $6\frac{1}{8}$ | 5.60 | $8\frac{1}{8}$ | 7.43 |
| $\frac{1}{2}$ | 13 | 1.3 | 12 | 30.5 | 33 | 83.8 | $\frac{1}{4}$ | 0.23 | $2\frac{1}{4}$ | 2.06 | $4\frac{1}{4}$ | 3.89 | $6\frac{1}{4}$ | 5.72 | $8\frac{1}{4}$ | 7.54 |
| $\frac{5}{8}$ | 16 | 1.6 | 13 | 33.0 | 34 | 86.4 | $\frac{3}{8}$ | 0.34 | $2\frac{3}{8}$ | 2.17 | $4\frac{3}{8}$ | 4.00 | $6\frac{3}{8}$ | 5.83 | $8\frac{3}{8}$ | 7.66 |
| $\frac{3}{4}$ | 19 | 1.9 | 14 | 35.6 | 35 | 88.9 | $\frac{1}{2}$ | 0.46 | $2\frac{1}{2}$ | 2.29 | $4\frac{1}{2}$ | 4.11 | $6\frac{1}{2}$ | 5.94 | $8\frac{1}{2}$ | 7.77 |
| $\frac{7}{8}$ | 22 | 2.2 | 15 | 38.1 | 36 | 91.4 | $\frac{5}{8}$ | 0.57 | $2\frac{5}{8}$ | 2.40 | $4\frac{5}{8}$ | 4.23 | $6\frac{5}{8}$ | 6.06 | $8\frac{5}{8}$ | 7.89 |
| 1 | 25 | 2.5 | 16 | 40.6 | 37 | 94.0 | $\frac{3}{4}$ | 0.69 | $2\frac{3}{4}$ | 2.51 | $4\frac{3}{4}$ | 4.34 | $6\frac{3}{4}$ | 6.17 | $8\frac{3}{4}$ | 8.00 |
| $1\frac{1}{4}$ | 32 | 3.2 | 17 | 43.2 | 38 | 96.5 | $\frac{7}{8}$ | 0.80 | $2\frac{7}{8}$ | 2.63 | $4\frac{7}{8}$ | 4.46 | $6\frac{7}{8}$ | 6.29 | $8\frac{7}{8}$ | 8.12 |
| $1\frac{1}{2}$ | 38 | 3.8 | 18 | 45.7 | 39 | 99.1 | 1 | 0.91 | 3 | 2.74 | 5 | 4.57 | 7 | 6.40 | 9 | 8.23 |
| $1\frac{3}{4}$ | 44 | 4.4 | 19 | 48.3 | 40 | 101.6 | $1\frac{1}{8}$ | 1.03 | $3\frac{1}{8}$ | 2.86 | $5\frac{1}{8}$ | 4.69 | $7\frac{1}{8}$ | 6.52 | $9\frac{1}{8}$ | 8.34 |
| 2 | 51 | 5.1 | 20 | 50.8 | 41 | 104.1 | $1\frac{1}{4}$ | 1.14 | $3\frac{1}{4}$ | 2.97 | $5\frac{1}{4}$ | 4.80 | $7\frac{1}{4}$ | 6.63 | $9\frac{1}{4}$ | 8.46 |
| $2\frac{1}{2}$ | 64 | 6.4 | 21 | 53.3 | 42 | 106.7 | $1\frac{3}{8}$ | 1.26 | $3\frac{3}{8}$ | 3.09 | $5\frac{3}{8}$ | 4.91 | $7\frac{3}{8}$ | 6.74 | $9\frac{3}{8}$ | 8.57 |
| 3 | 76 | 7.6 | 22 | 55.9 | 43 | 109.2 | $1\frac{1}{2}$ | 1.37 | $3\frac{1}{2}$ | 3.20 | $5\frac{1}{2}$ | 5.03 | $7\frac{1}{2}$ | 6.86 | $9\frac{1}{2}$ | 8.69 |
| $3\frac{1}{2}$ | 89 | 8.9 | 23 | 58.4 | 44 | 111.8 | $1\frac{5}{8}$ | 1.49 | $3\frac{5}{8}$ | 3.31 | $5\frac{5}{8}$ | 5.14 | $7\frac{5}{8}$ | 6.97 | $9\frac{5}{8}$ | 8.80 |
| 4 | 102 | 10.2 | 24 | 61.0 | 45 | 114.3 | $1\frac{3}{4}$ | 1.60 | $3\frac{3}{4}$ | 3.43 | $5\frac{3}{4}$ | 5.26 | $7\frac{3}{4}$ | 7.09 | $9\frac{3}{4}$ | 8.92 |
| $4\frac{1}{2}$ | 114 | 11.4 | 25 | 63.5 | 46 | 116.8 | $1\frac{7}{8}$ | 1.71 | $3\frac{7}{8}$ | 3.54 | $5\frac{7}{8}$ | 5.37 | $7\frac{7}{8}$ | 7.20 | $9\frac{7}{8}$ | 9.03 |
| 5 | 127 | 12.7 | 26 | 66.0 | 47 | 119.4 | 2 | 1.83 | 4 | 3.66 | 6 | 5.49 | 8 | 7.32 | 10 | 9.14 |
| 6 | 152 | 15.2 | 27 | 68.6 | 48 | 121.9 | | | | | | | | | | |
| 7 | 178 | 17.8 | 28 | 71.1 | 49 | 124.5 | | | | | | | | | | |
| 8 | 203 | 20.3 | 29 | 73.7 | 50 | 127.0 | | | | | | | | | | |

# index